CREATE

ONE-YEAR BLOG & EDITORIAL PLANNER

Create Exceptional Content, Get More Done and
Smash Through Your Blogging Goals

MEERA KOTHAND

My Queen,

I truly believe in you ability to make change, and inspire ~~others~~. I am here to support you through all your goals and dreams.

I love you!
Merry Christmas

A III

CREATE
COPYRIGHT AND PERMISSIONS

Where Marketing Meets Simple So That Bloggers And Solopreneurs Can Build
An Unmissable Stand Out Online Presence Minus The Sleaze

© 2017 MEERA KOTHAND

COPYRIGHT

All rights reserved. No part of this publication may be reproduced, distributed, stored in a retrieval system, or transmitted in any form or by any means, including photocopying, recording, or other electronic or mechanical methods, without the prior written permission of the publisher, except in the case of brief quotations embodied in critical reviews and certain other noncommercial uses permitted by copyright law.

While the publisher and author have used their best efforts in preparing this guide and planner, they make no representations or warranties with respect to the accuracy or completeness of the contents of this document. The information is to be used at your own risk. Every situation is different and will not be an exact replica of the examples given in this eBook. The author cannot guarantee results or any specific outcomes gleaned from using the methods outlined in the following pages.

PERMISSIONS

You have permission to photograph this planner for your review and include any photographs or videos in your social media sharing. Please do not photograph and/or film the whole planner.

For other permission requests, please email the author: **meera@meerakothand.com**

CONTENTS PAGE

Before we dive in, go to CREATEPLANNER.COM/BONUS
to download the bonuses that go along with this book.

MAKE SURE YOU VISUALIZE WHAT YOU REALLY WANT, NOT WHAT SOMEONE ELSE WANTS FOR YOU.

- JERRY GILLIES, AUTHOR

You're done.

You're done being ambushed by shiny-object syndrome, procrastination and over commitment.

You're ready for growth. You're ready to take your blog up a notch. You're ready to feel like you're *finally* in control of your blog and business.

Navigating everything you need to do *and* know to build a blog and business can be challenging and overwhelming.

Email, blog posts, social media, traffic, growing an audience - there are so many moving pieces and bringing it all together can seem like an impossible task.

As a full-time blogger, I found myself straddling a notebook for daily tasks , a huge desk calendar for promotions and launches, tracking my analytics in one and planning my content in another. It was confusing and frustrating.

After working with several clients and readers, I also realized that most bloggers and solopreneurs struggle to gain clarity on what to focus on and what to track.

But that's exactly what you need to do to get ahead. You can't be all over the place.

The bloggers who have the most success don't jump from one shiny object to the other. They don't try different tactics hoping one sticks. They have mapped out a larger picture of how their blog will grow. They have a plan of action.

And this is why I created the CREATE planner.

CREATE is a planning and editorial system designed specifically to help ambitious bloggers and solopreneurs like you create intentional content, grow and nurture an audience and build a business around your blog.

It combines everything I've learned from working with my clients as well as how I plan my own year – meshing content with strategy and purpose. This planner is for you if you're ready to hold yourself accountable, track your progress and make major strides in your blog and business.

And if you're here, you definitely are!

How the CREATE Planner Is Structured

The CREATE planner keeps you focused on your blogging goals by tracking and analyzing what matters most. It puts the right questions in front of you to help you understand your audience better and to create content designed to showcase your products and services.

With this planner, you'll see the big picture as well as zoom in and plan your blog at the granular level.

 The planner is undated so you can start using it at any time of the year. **'YOUR CREATE SPACES'** are blank pockets within the planner for you to brainstorm and jot down your ideas.

Here's how it works:

1. Plan your year with major dates and projects.

2. Set goals for the quarter.

3. Plan your months and days based on your goals and four main blogging tasks.

4. View your month at a glance.

5. Review your months and quarters to track the numbers that matter most and pick out patterns that give you an insight to your audience.

You have an overview of your entire year with spaces to lock in huge projects and important dates. You also have pages for each month where you work on content, email and detailed tasks. If you prefer an overview of the month in a two-page calendar, you have that too. The order of how you fill these in depends on how you like to plan.

I like to see an overview of the month by plotting in key dates into the monthly calendar. These key dates are what I'm launching for the month as well as affiliate and sales promotions. I then work backwards and flesh out the details - content, emails and other tasks. This helps me reverse engineer what I need to do to reach my goals.

You may decide to flesh out the content and details first before filling these into the monthly overview.

It's YOUR planner and YOU decide how you want to use it.

If you'd like to add a daily aspect to your planning, print the daily time sheet provided in the bonus pack.

The point of mapping out both the overview and details is to ensure that your goals and content are aligned with each other. It helps you work smarter so that you don't *ever* create content and send emails simply to fill your publishing schedule.

For instance, if you're launching an ebook this month on meal planning, your content for that month as well as the one prior to that needs to be centered around meal planning. It needs to focus on bringing attention to the problem your ebook is trying to solve, instilling desire for your solution and letting the reader know why she needs to take action. Your content positions your ebook as the perfect solution.

Do you see how this creates purposeful content?

The structure of this editorial planner will constantly remind you to create content around your goals.

The Best Part Though...

The planner introduces you to two main concepts which have helped skyrocket the growth of my blog in a single year - The 5 step planning process and 4 main blogging tasks.

With these two concepts, you'll chart a content and email strategy that gels with your business and blogging goals. Every decision you make will be calculated and intentional.

Here's a snapshot of some other components in this planner:

- ◯ Editorial Planning
- ◯ Email Marketing
- ◯ Growth review & tracking; and more.

By using this blog and editorial planner, you will accomplish more, feel a greater sense of satisfaction, and make progress towards this larger vision of what you want your blog to achieve. If you've ever felt anxious staring at a blank planner full of pages, CREATE will hold your hand through the process. You will get prompts and tips so you're never lost as to how to plan your months and quarters.

Don't let another month slip by where you miss the opportunity to connect with your audience and profit from your passion.

You'll be amazed at how far you've come in a year if you started taking action today.

Let's go!

START HERE

THE 5-STEP PLANNING PROCESS

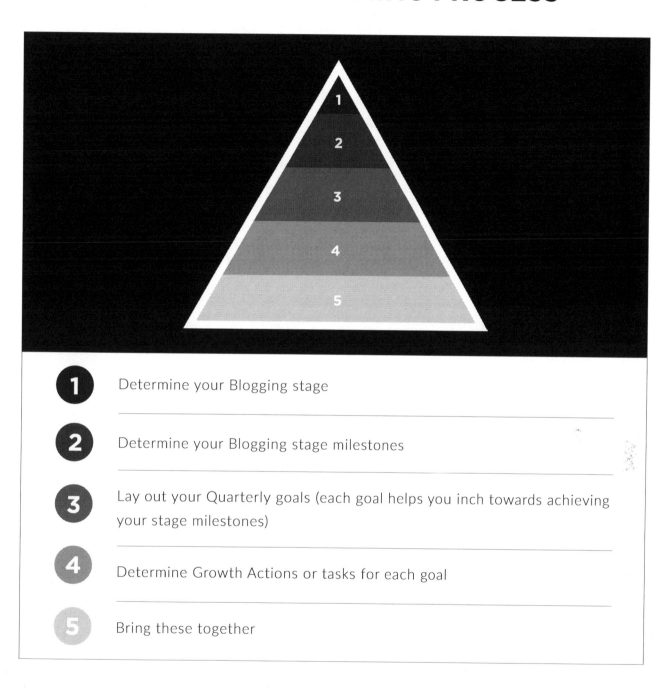

1. Determine your Blogging stage

2. Determine your Blogging stage milestones

3. Lay out your Quarterly goals (each goal helps you inch towards achieving your stage milestones)

4. Determine Growth Actions or tasks for each goal

5. Bring these together

Before we go into the 5-Step planning process, let's have a look at the different stages so you can determine where you are.

BUILDING YOUR ONLINE PLATFORM
- THE DIFFERENT STAGES

The table below gives an overview of the different stages in building your online platform and their respective milestones.

It's critical to tie your current blogging stage with your tasks and blogging goals. When the tasks you undertake are not aligned with your blogging stage, there's going to be a mismatch in your efforts and how much you get in return from them.

So, you need to focus only on tasks and goals that help you hit your most immediate milestone.

	STAGE 1	STAGE 2	STAGE 3	STAGE 4
MILESTONE	Launching your blog with a solid foundation	Nurture and grow your list to 500-1000 subscribers	Earn your first 1K	Earn a full-time income
HURDLE	Lack of clarity on what to do	Consistency and connecting with what your audience wants	Self-Doubt	Scaling and managing a team. Learning how to and what to outsource

A PRIMER FOR SETTING GOALS

Before you set any goal, ask yourself the following:

○ *Does it fit in with your blogging stage?*

Every goal you set and every task you do should be focused on reaching that end-point milestone. Everything that doesn't fit should be thrown out.

Likewise, if you're a course junkie and want to know when to invest in a course, check back with your blogging stage. Anything that doesn't move the needle for you at that moment is not a priority. Want to sign up for a webinar, ask yourself if this will help you reach your end-point milestone for the stage you're in.

If it does, sign up for it.
If it doesn't, don't.

○ *Is this a vanity metric or can it be broken down into growth actions and tasks you can directly influence? Is it possible to have a time or date stamp on each of these growth actions and tasks?*

What growth actions can you directly influence? Don't fall into the trap of vanity metrics. For instance have a look at this:

Quarter 1 Goals

Increase email list to 500 subscribers
Make first $200-$500

You can't influence these directly. But here's what you *can* influence:

Actions based on Goal 1

○ I will make an additional opt-in incentive
○ I will guest post on four blogs by the end of the quarter
○ I will run one promoted pin campaign

Actions based on Goal 2

○ I will write two detailed tutorials on my chosen affiliate product
○ I will update the affiliate links in my old posts
○ I will make a bonus ebook for subscribers who purchase through my affiliate link

See the difference?

When you break down your goals in this way and focus on growth actions you can directly influence, your goal immediately becomes attainable because you know exactly how you're going to get there.

Note I recommend picking only two-three goals per quarter. To see results you would need at least a solid quarter to work through these goals.

THE 4 MAJOR BLOGGING TASKS

How do you know what to spend your time on every day? What blogging tasks do you concentrate on? What's important and what's not?

I've read several articles and tried several iterations trying to optimize my schedule and it boils down to four main blogging tasks:

- ○ **Project tasks**
- ○ **Marketing tasks**
- ○ **Non-negotiable tasks**
- ○ **Web Optimization/design tasks**

Having four major blogging tasks to focus on stops you from multitasking. If you think that your energy and resources are split 50-50 when you work on two different tasks, you're wrong. Switching between tasks sucks up time and energy because the brain has to recall instructions on how to do a previous task before getting into the swing of things.

Let me break each of these down, and I'll show you how they come together in a calendar.

Project

Projects are usually bigger tasks such as working on an info product, creating a new opt-in incentive, working on your email sequence, writing a sales page, setting up your membership site, creating a media kit, working on a resource guide for your email list or recording videos for a course. Projects give you a higher impact and return at the end.

These are usually tasks that will benefit from a sprint.

A sprint is where you focus on one activity for a short period of time so you can get more of it done.

A sprint may stretch for a week or more. It helps you focus on your project and ship it out fast.

Marketing or promotional tasks

When you're so engrossed in your blog and struggle to keep up with social media and producing content, marketing is the one that takes a back seat. If no one knows your blog exists, it doesn't matter even if you create exceptional content. This is why marketing and promoting your blog is so important.

When I talk about marketing, I'm not just talking about scheduling your posts on social media or posting in Facebook groups. These are tasks that usually involve pitching your services to another party or getting in touch with someone to build a relationship. These tasks help to get your name and blog out there.

Here are examples of marketing or promotional activities:

- ◯ Pitching a sponsored post
- ◯ Pitching a guest post
- ◯ Pitching a podcast
- ◯ Offering suggestions to influencers
- ◯ Offering to teach someone's audience for free
- ◯ Gaining visibility in popular Facebook groups

Maintenance tasks/Web optimization/Design tasks

This is another area that gets pushed to the bottom of the list unknowingly. There are always little things you can do to optimize your website.

I usually try to schedule one web optimization or design task per week. This week, I can work on putting some testimonials and 'as seen in' logos on some of my landing pages. On other weeks I refresh my resources page or about page. Do you need to add an exit intent pop-up? That's a web optimization task as well.

Here are a few other examples:

- ○ Compress images using tiny png
- ○ Prepare vertical images for old posts
- ○ Optimize Pinterest descriptions
- ○ Amend 'about' sidebar blurb
- ○ Add opt-in forms in footer and top bar
- ○ Optimize opt-in forms to add logos and testimonials
- ○ Make cover image consistent across social media profiles

I always have a running list of tasks that I can dip into for each week. I have shared that list with you as well in the BONUS section. If I skip my schedule and haven't done these in a while, I put all my design tasks together and do them as a major project which spans the entire week.

Non-negotiable or bread and butter tasks

These are tasks that you *have* to do. They stay fixed on my schedule.

I rarely move them around unless I absolutely have to. I keep them fixed because if I move them around they don't get done.

Here are some examples:

- ○ Social media scheduling
- ○ Refilling Tailwind or Board booster
- ○ Facebook promo threads
- ○ Replying to subscriber emails
- ○ Replying to blog post comments
- ○ Replying to twitter mentions

Don't let the names of the different tasks confuse you. This just gives you an order and structure to follow so that nothing falls through the cracks when you're growing your blog.

Bringing the four blogging tasks together

Now that we've looked at the major blogging tasks, let me show you how they come together.

I use time blocking to structure my week. It starts with identifying your most productive time block.

Mine is 2-4pm. Everything just kicks into gear for me at this time. Once you identify this, schedule project tasks here. Here's a snapshot of my schedule and how the four tasks integrate into a calendar.

8-9am: Marketing Tasks
9-10am: Non-negotiable Tasks
2-4pm: Project Tasks

Your schedule will vary a lot from mine.

Identify what your major time blocks are by shading in the diagram. If yours varies day to day, draw the time circle into your daily calendar or use the daily time sheet given in the bonus pack.

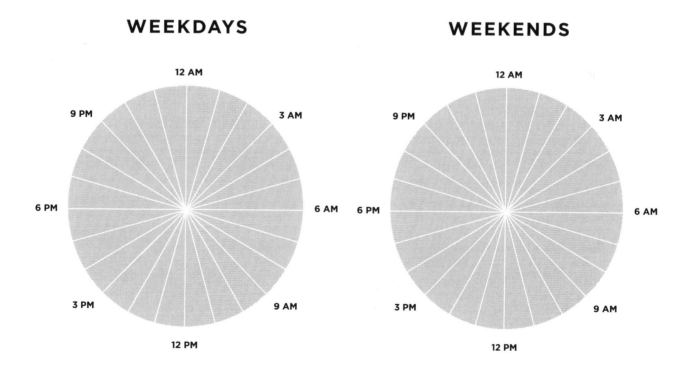

WEEKDAYS

WEEKENDS

YOUR MAIN PILLARS: CONTENT + EMAIL

CONTENT STRATEGY

Your content is the hub that attracts your target audience to your blog. Your content has to educate, entertain and inspire your readers in some way. Yours could do a mixture of all three.

You also want to create content that attracts your target audience and sells your products and services for you. This is what purposeful content does.

To start creating purposeful content and planning your content strategy, you need to know how your blog is going to help your reader.

This is where your blog value proposition comes in. It forms the basis for every single piece of content you create. How can you come up with an all-encompassing purpose or value proposition for your blog?

First, answer these two questions:

- What group do you want to help?
- In what area do you want to help them? Or what area do they struggle with that you believe you could help them in?

For example, let's say I want to help women. The topic I want to help them with is 'starting a home business'.

Now you have two areas to work with. Break this down further. Try to get specific with your answers. You're not helping all women, but single moms. And not just any type of home business, but a virtual assistant (VA) business.

Once you break it down in this way, your content angle takes on a very different dimension. Content for a single mom with two kids trying to run a home-based VA business is very different from content for a 20-something out of college trying to run a home-based VA business.

Then plot your answers into one of these two statements. Do this exercise for your blog right now.

I educate/inspire/entertain/teach/help ....

.... who want to ....

I show .... how ....

....

Examples:

○   I help single moms who want to build a successful VA business

○   I inspire 20-somethings to travel the world on a shoe-string budget

○   I show food bloggers how easy it is to take their own pictures and edit them

Now that you're clear about how you're helping them, let's dive deeper!

What content categories will support this purpose?

You know the end-point. You know how you're going to help your reader. But your content has to lead them there. Each category supports your overall purpose. And within each category you have sub-categories and topics.

To know your sub-categories, ask yourself what the reader needs to know to become well-versed in the category. Likewise, when you're fleshing out blog posts for each sub-category, ask yourself what the reader needs to know to become well-versed in the sub-category.

Let's take a website for moms who are attempting to build a home VA business. The categories could be:

○ Marketing yourself
○ Dealing with clients
○ Pricing your services

Let's break it up into Category > Sub-Category > Blog posts

Category - Marketing yourself

Ask yourself - What does the reader need to know to become an expert or to become proficient in this category

I have two sub-categories at this moment:

1. How to write a pitch
2. How to have a good website

Let's break each of these sub-categories down.

Sub-category 1
How to write a pitch

Ask yourself: What does the reader need to know to become an expert or to become proficient in this sub-category

Blog Posts:
• Should you cold pitch your VA services?
• 20 essential elements that make a killer pitch.

Sub-category 2
How to have a good writer website

Ask yourself: What does the reader need to know to become an expert or to become proficient in this sub-category

Blog Posts:
• 5 Essential components of a freelance writer website.
• 10 types of testimonials you need to have before pitching a high net worth client.

You can expand and dive deeper into each of your categories and sub-categories. This system will give you an endless list of blog post ideas to work with at any one time.

Now list out the content categories that will support your blog's purpose. You don't have to fill in all six blocks. Three categories are perfect to start with. You'd rather go narrow and deep with your content than wide and shallow.

Planning content around your products and services

Each one of your products and services helps the reader solve a problem or provides support for a pain point. But what does the reader need to be aware of before they are ready to purchase your products and engage your services?

They need to be aware of the problem your product is solving. Why it needs to be solved. How much better their lives would be and the benefits of solving the problem. Finally, they need to know how your product and service fits into the puzzle.

But you'll get readers who are at different ends of the spectrum. Some may have no clue about the problem you are solving. Some may be actively searching for a solution to it and comparing different products and services in the market. Different content pieces will appeal to these different readers.

For instance, let's take the example of the mom who wants to start a VA business. Let's say you have a coaching program that mentors them and guides them through the process. Here are some topics to serve readers at different stages:

- Why a VA business is perfect for moms and why you need to start one today - Unaware

- 13 things holding you back from launching your VA business - Problem Aware

- Think you have no skills to start a VA business? Think again. Here's why you may be perfect for the role -Problem Aware

- How a mastermind helped me launch my VA business in 2 weeks - Solution Unaware

- How this mom makes 10K a month from her VA business - Desire

Create content that walks the reader through each of these points. This gives you a framework to plan your content around your products, services and launches. Use this framework as you work your way through the planner.

Want to explore these ideas further? Check out the One Hour Content Plan at 1HCP.ME

EMAIL STRATEGY

There's a lot of emphasis on your email list in this planner.

That's because you own your email list. An email subscriber is more valuable than a social media follower. If you nurture your email subscribers with valuable content, they will be the biggest supporters of your products and services.

But apart from growing your email list, you need to think about the aims and goals you have for your list as well. This is not just about the tangible results like money, open rates or click rates. These are important, but you also need to consider the intangible aspects. The impact you want to have on your list and the feelings you want to evoke in your subscribers.

Take a moment now to think through the questions below. This will set a foundation for the type of emails you want to send and how you want to treat your email list and subscribers.

What do you want your subscribers to experience from your emails? how do you want them to feel?

Example: Like a friend who has their back, like they've found a mentor and leader, that you made their life easy with hacks and tips, that you've given them a new way of thinking about a topic?

Note There are dedicated areas within the planner to chart your email content and track opens and best performing subject lines. This will help you gain insight to your audience's preferences and behaviors.

What do you hope to get out of it for yourself?

Example: Do you want to be seen as an expert? Do you want to spread your love about a particular subject? Do you want to inspire a community?

What type of emails do you see yourself sending?

Example: Curated newsletters, tips, stories, how-to?

What metric will you use to track your progress? Opens? Clicks? Testimonials? Feedback?

Example: What's more important to you? If you have a lot of affiliate links in your curated newsletter, clicks may be more important to you. If your emails talk about how tos and perspectives, opens or feedback may be a better metric.

How often do you want to send out your emails?

I recommend once a week or fortnightly, but start with what you can and be consistent.

What time and when do you plan to send out your emails?

If you want to kick start your email list, sign up for my free email course 'Email Lists for Newbies' here: **WWW.MEERA.EMAIL/COURSE**

Terms Used In This Planner

CONTENT UPGRADES – A free resource or add-on content you offer with your blog post in exchange for your readers' email address

OPT-IN INCENTIVE – A free resource (cheat sheet, worksheet, guide, checklist) you offer in exchange for your readers' email address

COLD SUBSCRIBERS – Subscribers who haven't opened or engaged with your emails in a certain period of time; usually 3-6 months

RE-ENGAGEMENT CAMPAIGN – This is a series of 2-3 emails you send your 'cold' subscribers in an effort to discern their interest in staying on your list

CLEAN YOUR LIST – Every quarter, the planner prompts you to consider cleaning your list. A bigger list isn't necessarily better. For various reasons, many email subscribers stop opening and engaging with your emails after a certain period of time. You pay for every subscriber on your list and it's good practice to either re-engage these 'cold' subscribers or delete them off your list.

LANDING PAGE – A distraction-free page with no navigation bar or external links with a single goal of getting a reader to sign-up to your opt-in form

CONVERSION RATE – How many people signed-up on your opt-in form or landing page as a percentage of the total number of people who visited that opt-in form or landing page

With this foundation in place, it's now time to start planning and creating compelling content!

SHARE YOUR PROGRESS!

You're equipped with everything you need to make the best use of this planner and I can't wait to see what you create. I hope you'll share your progress with me on social media **@MEERAKOTHAND**.

Let's get going!

YOUR YEAR AT A GLANCE

What new products do you want to create this year?

_____
_____
_____
_____
_____
_____
_____
_____
_____
_____
_____

What new services do you want to offer this year?

_____
_____
_____
_____
_____
_____
_____
_____
_____
_____
_____

What will you do to grow your community and audience this year?

_____
_____
_____
_____
_____
_____
_____
_____

What's on your course/self-development/product wish list?

Before you answer this, consider the following questions:

Will it move your blog + business forward?

If you're not tech or design savvy and it's an element that's holding your business back, you may want to invest in tools that make design and tech easier for you.

Will it save you time?

If you're a fashion or food blogger and you rely on Instagram heavily as a platform to connect with your audience, you may want to invest in a scheduling tool like Grum to save you time.

Is there a deal or special discount? Is there a recurring fee?

Recurring fees are charged every month. If there is a similar product with a flat fee, do a comparison to see which is better.

Is it relevant for the stage you are in?

Will you have time to implement and put into practice what you learn in the course? Is this something you need for the stage you are in? If the answer is no, consider whether you really need this course at this point in time.

Name of Course/Product	Tentative Launch/Buy Date	Cost

Where do you want your brand to be featured?

List publications, websites and podcasts you want to target.

Who do you want to work with or collaborate with this year?

This list could also have names of influencers you want to connect and build a relationship with.

Name of Person/Brand	Site/URL	Potential Project/Idea

What's your revenue goal for the year?

Revenue is the sum total of what your business/blog generates in earnings. **Income** is your personal paycheck. It's the money in the business you send back to yourself in exchange for the work you do. If you are paying yourself a monthly income, add it into the table above.

Product: ....
....

Copies sold	Revenue

Product: ....
....

Copies sold	Revenue

Product: ....
....

Copies sold	Revenue

Income

Revenue

Affiliate Marketing Revenue	Sponsored Posts Revenue	Services Revenue
Source 1:	Source 1:	Source 1:
Source 2:	Source 2:	Source 2:
Source 3:	Source 3:	Source 3:
Source 4:	Source 4:	Source 4:
Source 5:	Source 5:	Source 5:
Source 6:	Source 6:	Source 6:

REVENUE

Estimated Blog Expenses for the Year
(Hosting, Email Service Provider Etc)

Expense	Amount

What goals or objectives, when achieved, will make your blog and business look like an absolute success this year?

1	2
3	4
5	6

Plug in your big projects, promotions and tentative launches into months.

January	February	March

April	May	June

July	August	September

October	November	December

Based on these key project and dates, what theme(s) will your content have for each month of the year? Content refers to blog posts, videos, emails etc.

Month: ....

Theme: ....

Month: ....

Theme: ....

Month: ....

Theme: ....

Month: ....

Theme: ....

Month: ....

Theme: ....

Month: ....

Theme: ....

Month: ....

Theme: ....

Month: ....

Theme: ....

Month: ....

Theme: ....

Month: ....

Theme: ....

Month: ....

Theme: ....

Month: ....

Theme: ....

PLAN YOUR QUARTER 1

What blogging stage are you in?

Stage 1   Stage 2   Stage 3   Stage 4

List 3 goals you want to achieve by the end of this quarter. Does every goal help you reach your stage milestone? If it doesn't, rethink your goal.

GOAL 1

LIST EVERY TASK YOU CAN THINK OF TO COMPLETE YOUR GOAL

GOAL 2

LIST EVERY TASK YOU CAN THINK OF TO COMPLETE YOUR GOAL

GOAL 3 ....

LIST EVERY TASK YOU CAN THINK OF TO COMPLETE YOUR GOAL

List any key projects and their deadlines for this quarter

Project	Deadline	Sprint Y/N	Tentative Sprint Dates

LET'S PLAN MONTH:

List 3 things you hope to achieve by the end of the month?

GOAL 1

LIST EVERY TASK YOU CAN THINK OF TO COMPLETE YOUR GOAL

GOAL 2

LIST EVERY TASK YOU CAN THINK OF TO COMPLETE YOUR GOAL

GOAL 3

LIST EVERY TASK YOU CAN THINK OF TO COMPLETE YOUR GOAL

List All Maintenance Tasks for the Month

○ *E.g. Redo Homepage* ....

○ ....

○ ....

○ ....

○ ....

○ ....

○ ....

○ ....

○ ....

List All Marketing Tasks for the Month

○ *E.g. Pitch Podcast X* ....

○ ....

○ ....

○ ....

○ ....

○ ....

○ ....

○ ....

○ ....

List All Project Tasks for the Month

○ .... ○ ....

○ .... ○ ....

○ .... ○ ....

○ .... ○ ....

List Important Dates for the Month

List all launch dates, affiliate promotions, collaborations, sales etc.

○ .... ○ ....

○ .... ○ ....

○ .... ○ ....

○ .... ○ ....

What content would support your goals for this month?

What content upgrades would complement these posts?

YOUR CREATE SPACE

What content do you plan to publish this month?

Include any audios and videos as well. Plot your content ideas into this table.

Date	Title	Format
14.03.18	Why you need a content plan: 5 Steps to Create your brilliant content plan	Blog post

Goal of Content	Content Upgrade	Outline	Draft	Edit	Publish
Awareness - why a content plan is important	Checklist	○	○	⊗	○
		○	○	○	○
		○	○	○	○
		○	○	○	○
		○	○	○	○
		○	○	○	○
		○	○	○	○
		○	○	○	○
		○	○	○	○
		○	○	○	○
		○	○	○	○
		○	○	○	○
		○	○	○	○
		○	○	○	○
		○	○	○	○
		○	○	○	○
		○	○	○	○
		○	○	○	○
		○	○	○	○
		○	○	○	○
		○	○	○	○
		○	○	○	○
		○	○	○	○

What emails will you send this month?

Think about the type of email content that will support your goals for this month.
Brainstorm at least 3 subject lines for each email.

Gist of Email Content	Subject Line(s)

Goal/Call to Action in Email	Send Date	Outline	Draft	Edit	Scheduled
		○	○	○	○
		○	○	○	○
		○	○	○	○
		○	○	○	○
		○	○	○	○
		○	○	○	○
		○	○	○	○
		○	○	○	○
		○	○	○	○
		○	○	○	○
		○	○	○	○
		○	○	○	○
		○	○	○	○
		○	○	○	○
		○	○	○	○
		○	○	○	○
		○	○	○	○
		○	○	○	○
		○	○	○	○
		○	○	○	○
		○	○	○	○

MONTH AT A GLANCE

SUNDAY	MONDAY	TUESDAY	WEDNESDAY

Plug your tasks, key dates and projects for the month into the overview.
Are you doing a sprint? Block it off in the calendar.

THURSDAY	FRIDAY	SATURDAY	NOTES

REVIEW YOUR MONTH

	This Month	Last Month	+/- Change
Email Subscribers			
Pageviews			
Bounce Rate			
5 Most Popular Posts (In Google Analytics)			
Average session time			
Top 5 Traffic Refferers			

Track each of your emails sent out this month.

Subject Line	Open Rate	Click Rate

Revenue Source	Amount
Total	

Expenses	Amount
Total	

	This Month	Last Month	+/- Change
f			
🐦			
📷			
in			
g+			
📌			
▶			

Track each post for the month and how well it did on two of your most important social media platforms. Track the number of opt-ins each content upgrade received.

Posts	Social Shares	Content Upgrade Opt-ins	Comments

LET'S PLAN MONTH: ....

List 3 things you hope to achieve by the end of the month?

GOAL 1 ....

LIST EVERY TASK YOU CAN THINK OF TO COMPLETE YOUR GOAL

GOAL 2 ....

LIST EVERY TASK YOU CAN THINK OF TO COMPLETE YOUR GOAL

GOAL 3 ....

LIST EVERY TASK YOU CAN THINK OF TO COMPLETE YOUR GOAL

List All Maintenance Tasks for the Month

- ○ ....
- ○ ....
- ○ ....
- ○ ....
- ○ ....
- ○ ....
- ○ ....
- ○ ....
- ○ ....

List All Marketing Tasks for the Month

- ○ ....
- ○ ....
- ○ ....
- ○ ....
- ○ ....
- ○ ....
- ○ ....
- ○ ....
- ○ ....

List All Project Tasks for the Month

- ○ ....
- ○ ....
- ○ ....
- ○ ....

- ○ ....
- ○ ....
- ○ ....
- ○ ....

List Important Dates for the Month

List all launch dates, affiliate promotions, collaborations, sales etc.

- ○ ....
- ○ ....
- ○ ....
- ○ ....

- ○ ....
- ○ ....
- ○ ....
- ○ ....

YOUR CREATE SPACE

What content would support your goals for this month?

What content upgrades would complement these posts?

What content do you plan to publish this month?

Include any audios and videos as well. Plot your content ideas into this table.

Date	Title	Format

Goal of Content	Content Upgrade	Outline	Draft	Edit	Publish
		○	○	○	○
		○	○	○	○
		○	○	○	○
		○	○	○	○
		○	○	○	○
		○	○	○	○
		○	○	○	○
		○	○	○	○
		○	○	○	○
		○	○	○	○
		○	○	○	○
		○	○	○	○
		○	○	○	○
		○	○	○	○
		○	○	○	○
		○	○	○	○
		○	○	○	○
		○	○	○	○
		○	○	○	○
		○	○	○	○
		○	○	○	○
		○	○	○	○
		○	○	○	○
		○	○	○	○

What emails will you send this month?

Think about the type of email content that will support your goals for this month.
Brainstorm at least 3 subject lines for each email.

Gist of Email Content	Subject Line(s)

Goal/Call to Action in Email	Send Date	Outline	Draft	Edit	Scheduled
		◯	◯	◯	◯
		◯	◯	◯	◯
		◯	◯	◯	◯
		◯	◯	◯	◯
		◯	◯	◯	◯
		◯	◯	◯	◯
		◯	◯	◯	◯
		◯	◯	◯	◯
		◯	◯	◯	◯
		◯	◯	◯	◯
		◯	◯	◯	◯
		◯	◯	◯	◯
		◯	◯	◯	◯
		◯	◯	◯	◯
		◯	◯	◯	◯
		◯	◯	◯	◯
		◯	◯	◯	◯
		◯	◯	◯	◯
		◯	◯	◯	◯
		◯	◯	◯	◯
		◯	◯	◯	◯

MONTH AT A GLANCE

SUNDAY	MONDAY	TUESDAY	WEDNESDAY

Plug your tasks, key dates and projects for the month into the overview.
Are you doing a sprint? Block it off in the calendar.

THURSDAY	FRIDAY	SATURDAY	NOTES

REVIEW YOUR MONTH

	This Month	Last Month	+/- Change
Email Subscribers			
Pageviews			
Bounce Rate			
5 Most Popular Posts (In Google Analytics)			
Average session time			
Top 5 Traffic Refferers			

Track each of your emails sent out this month.

Subject Line	Open Rate	Click Rate

Revenue Source	Amount
Total	

Expenses	Amount
Total	

	This Month	Last Month	+/- Change
f			
t			
insta			
in			
g+			
p			
yt			

Track each post for the month and how well it did on two of your most important social media platforms. Track the number of opt-ins each content upgrade received.

Posts	Social Shares	Content Upgrade Opt-ins	Comments

LET'S PLAN MONTH:

List 3 things you hope to achieve by the end of the month?

GOAL 1

LIST EVERY TASK YOU CAN THINK OF TO COMPLETE YOUR GOAL

GOAL 2

LIST EVERY TASK YOU CAN THINK OF TO COMPLETE YOUR GOAL

GOAL 3

LIST EVERY TASK YOU CAN THINK OF TO COMPLETE YOUR GOAL

List All Maintenance Tasks for the Month

○ ....
○ ....
○ ....
○ ....
○ ....
○ ....
○ ....
○ ....
○ ....

List All Marketing Tasks for the Month

○ ....
○ ....
○ ....
○ ....
○ ....
○ ....
○ ....
○ ....
○ ....

List All Project Tasks for the Month

○ ....   ○ ....
○ ....   ○ ....
○ ....   ○ ....
○ ....   ○ ....

List Important Dates for the Month

List all launch dates, affiliate promotions, collaborations, sales etc.

○ ....   ○ ....
○ ....   ○ ....
○ ....   ○ ....
○ ....   ○ ....

What content would support your goals for this month?

What content upgrades would complement these posts?

What content do you plan to publish this month?

Include any audios and videos as well. Plot your content ideas into this table.

Date	Title	Format

Goal of Content	Content Upgrade	Outline	Draft	Edit	Publish
		○	○	○	○
		○	○	○	○
		○	○	○	○
		○	○	○	○
		○	○	○	○
		○	○	○	○
		○	○	○	○
		○	○	○	○
		○	○	○	○
		○	○	○	○
		○	○	○	○
		○	○	○	○
		○	○	○	○
		○	○	○	○
		○	○	○	○
		○	○	○	○
		○	○	○	○
		○	○	○	○
		○	○	○	○
		○	○	○	○
		○	○	○	○
		○	○	○	○
		○	○	○	○
		○	○	○	○

What emails will you send this month?

Think about the type of email content that will support your goals for this month.
Brainstorm at least 3 subject lines for each email.

Gist of Email Content	Subject Line(s)

Goal/Call to Action in Email	Send Date	Outline	Draft	Edit	Scheduled
		◯	◯	◯	◯
		◯	◯	◯	◯
		◯	◯	◯	◯
		◯	◯	◯	◯
		◯	◯	◯	◯
		◯	◯	◯	◯
		◯	◯	◯	◯
		◯	◯	◯	◯
		◯	◯	◯	◯
		◯	◯	◯	◯
		◯	◯	◯	◯
		◯	◯	◯	◯
		◯	◯	◯	◯
		◯	◯	◯	◯
		◯	◯	◯	◯
		◯	◯	◯	◯
		◯	◯	◯	◯
		◯	◯	◯	◯
		◯	◯	◯	◯
		◯	◯	◯	◯
		◯	◯	◯	◯

MONTH AT A GLANCE

SUNDAY	MONDAY	TUESDAY	WEDNESDAY

Plug your tasks, key dates and projects for the month into the overview.
Are you doing a sprint? Block it off in the calendar.

THURSDAY	FRIDAY	SATURDAY	NOTES

REVIEW YOUR MONTH

	This Month	Last Month	+/- Change
Email Subscribers			
Pageviews			
Bounce Rate			
5 Most Popular Posts (In Google Analytics)			
Average session time			
Top 5 Traffic Refferers			

Track each of your emails sent out this month.

Subject Line	Open Rate	Click Rate

Revenue Source	Amount
Total	

Expenses	Amount
Total	

	This Month	Last Month	+/- Change
f			
(Twitter)			
(Instagram)			
in			
g+			
p			
(YouTube)			

Track each post for the month and how well it did on two of your most important social media platforms. Track the number of opt-ins each content upgrade received.

Posts	Social Shares	Content Upgrade Opt-ins	Comments

REVIEW YOUR QUARTER 1

What worked well for you this quarter?

How can you replicate these results?

What obstacles are you facing in achieving your goals? Why is it difficult?

Did this quarter help you get closer to your annual objectives?

What can you try to overcome them?

List Your Top 5 Most Popular Content Upgrades for this Quarter	Subscribers

Let's review your content strategy for the quarter:

Do you see any patterns in the type of posts that attract an audience to your blog?

How can you capitalize on the success of these posts? (Example: Add content upgrades, develop a related product, create similar posts, repurpose existing posts)

Let's review your email strategy for the quarter:

Do you see any patterns in the type of subject lines that worked well for your list?

Which emails received the most engagement and replies from your list? Can you tell why?

What opt-in incentive is working in terms of conversion rate? Keep it status quo or change it up?

_____
_____
_____
_____

Do you need to clean your list? (Re-engage or delete subscribers who haven't opened or clicked on your emails in 3 months or more)

_____
_____
_____
_____

Do you need to make changes to how your website is optimized? (E.g. Any posts with lots of traffic buy not converting to subscribers? Do you need to add extra opt-in forms? Do you need to add testimonials to a landing page?)

_____
_____
_____
_____

Are there any emails with a high unsubscribe rate? Can you tell why?

_____
_____
_____

Do you see any patterns in the type of content upgrades that get the most opt-ins?

_____
_____
_____

Where did most subscribers come from?

_____
_____
_____

PLAN YOUR QUARTER 2

What blogging stage are you in?

List 3 goals you want to achieve by the end of this quarter. Does every goal help you reach your stage milestone? If it doesn't, rethink your goal.

GOAL 1 ....

LIST EVERY TASK YOU CAN THINK OF TO COMPLETE YOUR GOAL

GOAL 2 ....

LIST EVERY TASK YOU CAN THINK OF TO COMPLETE YOUR GOAL

GOAL 3 ....

List any key projects and their deadlines for this quarter

Project	Deadline	Sprint Y/N	Tentative Sprint Dates

LET'S PLAN MONTH:

List 3 things you hope to achieve by the end of the month?

GOAL 1

LIST EVERY TASK YOU CAN THINK OF TO COMPLETE YOUR GOAL

GOAL 2

LIST EVERY TASK YOU CAN THINK OF TO COMPLETE YOUR GOAL

GOAL 3

LIST EVERY TASK YOU CAN THINK OF TO COMPLETE YOUR GOAL

List All Maintenance Tasks for the Month

○ ....
○ ....
○ ....
○ ....
○ ....
○ ....
○ ....
○ ....
○ ....

List All Marketing Tasks for the Month

○ ....
○ ....
○ ....
○ ....
○ ....
○ ....
○ ....
○ ....
○ ....

List All Project Tasks for the Month

○ .... ○ ....
○ .... ○ ....
○ .... ○ ....
○ .... ○ ....

List Important Dates for the Month

List all launch dates, affiliate promotions, collaborations, sales etc.

○ .... ○ ....
○ .... ○ ....
○ .... ○ ....
○ .... ○ ....

What content would support your goals for this month?

What content upgrades would complement these posts?

What content do you plan to publish this month?

Include any audios and videos as well. Plot your content ideas into this table.

Date	Title	Format

Goal of Content	Content Upgrade	Outline	Draft	Edit	Publish
		○	○	○	○
		○	○	○	○
		○	○	○	○
		○	○	○	○
		○	○	○	○
		○	○	○	○
		○	○	○	○
		○	○	○	○
		○	○	○	○
		○	○	○	○
		○	○	○	○
		○	○	○	○
		○	○	○	○
		○	○	○	○
		○	○	○	○
		○	○	○	○
		○	○	○	○
		○	○	○	○
		○	○	○	○
		○	○	○	○
		○	○	○	○
		○	○	○	○
		○	○	○	○
		○	○	○	○

What emails will you send this month?

Think about the type of email content that will support your goals for this month.
Brainstorm at least 3 subject lines for each email.

Gist of Email Content	Subject Line(s)

Goal/Call to Action in Email	Send Date	Outline	Draft	Edit	Scheduled
		◯	◯	◯	◯
		◯	◯	◯	◯
		◯	◯	◯	◯
		◯	◯	◯	◯
		◯	◯	◯	◯
		◯	◯	◯	◯
		◯	◯	◯	◯
		◯	◯	◯	◯
		◯	◯	◯	◯
		◯	◯	◯	◯
		◯	◯	◯	◯
		◯	◯	◯	◯
		◯	◯	◯	◯
		◯	◯	◯	◯
		◯	◯	◯	◯
		◯	◯	◯	◯
		◯	◯	◯	◯
		◯	◯	◯	◯
		◯	◯	◯	◯
		◯	◯	◯	◯
		◯	◯	◯	◯

MONTH AT A GLANCE

SUNDAY	MONDAY	TUESDAY	WEDNESDAY

Plug your tasks, key dates and projects for the month into the overview.
Are you doing a sprint? Block it off in the calendar.

THURSDAY	FRIDAY	SATURDAY	NOTES

REVIEW YOUR MONTH

	This Month	Last Month	+/- Change
Email Subscribers			
Pageviews			
Bounce Rate			
5 Most Popular Posts (In Google Analytics)			
Average session time			
Top 5 Traffic Refferers			

Track each of your emails sent out this month.

Subject Line	Open Rate	Click Rate

Revenue Source	Amount
Total	

Expenses	Amount
Total	

	This Month	Last Month	+/- Change
f			
🐦			
📷			
in			
g+			
📌			
▶			

Track each post for the month and how well it did on two of your most important social media platforms. Track the number of opt-ins each content upgrade received.

Posts	Social Shares	Content Upgrade Opt-ins	Comments

LET'S PLAN MONTH:

List 3 things you hope to achieve by the end of the month?

GOAL 1

LIST EVERY TASK YOU CAN THINK OF TO COMPLETE YOUR GOAL

GOAL 2

LIST EVERY TASK YOU CAN THINK OF TO COMPLETE YOUR GOAL

GOAL 3

LIST EVERY TASK YOU CAN THINK OF TO COMPLETE YOUR GOAL

List All Maintenance Tasks for the Month

- ○ ....
- ○ ....
- ○ ....
- ○ ....
- ○ ....
- ○ ....
- ○ ....
- ○ ....
- ○ ....

List All Marketing Tasks for the Month

- ○ ....
- ○ ....
- ○ ....
- ○ ....
- ○ ....
- ○ ....
- ○ ....
- ○ ....
- ○ ....

List All Project Tasks for the Month

- ○ ....
- ○ ....
- ○ ....
- ○ ....

- ○ ....
- ○ ....
- ○ ....
- ○ ....

List Important Dates for the Month

List all launch dates, affiliate promotions, collaborations, sales etc.

- ○ ....
- ○ ....
- ○ ....
- ○ ....

- ○ ....
- ○ ....
- ○ ....
- ○ ....

What content would support your goals for this month?

What content upgrades would complement these posts?

YOUR CREATE SPACE

What content do you plan to publish this month?

Include any audios and videos as well. Plot your content ideas into this table.

Date	Title	Format

Goal of Content	Content Upgrade	Outline	Draft	Edit	Publish
---	---	:---::	:---:	:---:	:---:
		○	○	○	○
		○	○	○	○
		○	○	○	○
		○	○	○	○
		○	○	○	○
		○	○	○	○
		○	○	○	○
		○	○	○	○
		○	○	○	○
		○	○	○	○
		○	○	○	○
		○	○	○	○
		○	○	○	○
		○	○	○	○
		○	○	○	○
		○	○	○	○
		○	○	○	○
		○	○	○	○
		○	○	○	○
		○	○	○	○
		○	○	○	○
		○	○	○	○
		○	○	○	○

What emails will you send this month?

Think about the type of email content that will support your goals for this month. Brainstorm at least 3 subject lines for each email.

Gist of Email Content	Subject Line(s)

Goal/Call to Action in Email	Send Date	Outline	Draft	Edit	Scheduled
		○	○	○	○
		○	○	○	○
		○	○	○	○
		○	○	○	○
		○	○	○	○
		○	○	○	○
		○	○	○	○
		○	○	○	○
		○	○	○	○
		○	○	○	○
		○	○	○	○
		○	○	○	○
		○	○	○	○
		○	○	○	○
		○	○	○	○
		○	○	○	○
		○	○	○	○
		○	○	○	○
		○	○	○	○
		○	○	○	○
		○	○	○	○

MONTH AT A GLANCE

SUNDAY	MONDAY	TUESDAY	WEDNESDAY

Plug your tasks, key dates and projects for the month into the overview.
Are you doing a sprint? Block it off in the calendar.

THURSDAY	FRIDAY	SATURDAY	NOTES

REVIEW YOUR MONTH

	This Month	Last Month	+/- Change
Email Subscribers			
Pageviews			
Bounce Rate			
5 Most Popular Posts (In Google Analytics)			
Average session time			
Top 5 Traffic Refferers			

Track each of your emails sent out this month.

Subject Line	Open Rate	Click Rate

Revenue Source	Amount
Total	

Expenses	Amount
Total	

	This Month	Last Month	+/- Change
f			
(twitter)			
(instagram)			
in			
g+			
(pinterest)			
(youtube)			

Track each post for the month and how well it did on two of your most important social media platforms. Track the number of opt-ins each content upgrade received.

Posts	Social Shares	Content Upgrade Opt-ins	Comments

LET'S PLAN MONTH:

List 3 things you hope to achieve by the end of the month?

GOAL 1

LIST EVERY TASK YOU CAN THINK OF TO COMPLETE YOUR GOAL

GOAL 2

LIST EVERY TASK YOU CAN THINK OF TO COMPLETE YOUR GOAL

GOAL 3

LIST EVERY TASK YOU CAN THINK OF TO COMPLETE YOUR GOAL

List All Maintenance Tasks for the Month

- ○ ....
- ○ ....
- ○ ....
- ○ ....
- ○ ....
- ○ ....
- ○ ....
- ○ ....
- ○ ....

List All Marketing Tasks for the Month

- ○ ....
- ○ ....
- ○ ....
- ○ ....
- ○ ....
- ○ ....
- ○ ....
- ○ ....
- ○ ....

List All Project Tasks for the Month

- ○ ....
- ○ ....
- ○ ....
- ○ ....

- ○ ....
- ○ ....
- ○ ....
- ○ ....

List Important Dates for the Month

List all launch dates, affiliate promotions, collaborations, sales etc.

- ○ ....
- ○ ....
- ○ ....
- ○ ....

- ○ ....
- ○ ....
- ○ ....
- ○ ....

What content would support your goals for this month?

What content upgrades would complement these posts?

What content do you plan to publish this month?

Include any audios and videos as well. Plot your content ideas into this table.

Date	Title	Format

Goal of Content	Content Upgrade	Outline	Draft	Edit	Publish
		○	○	○	○
		○	○	○	○
		○	○	○	○
		○	○	○	○
		○	○	○	○
		○	○	○	○
		○	○	○	○
		○	○	○	○
		○	○	○	○
		○	○	○	○
		○	○	○	○
		○	○	○	○
		○	○	○	○
		○	○	○	○
		○	○	○	○
		○	○	○	○
		○	○	○	○
		○	○	○	○
		○	○	○	○
		○	○	○	○
		○	○	○	○
		○	○	○	○
		○	○	○	○
		○	○	○	○

What emails will you send this month?

Think about the type of email content that will support your goals for this month.
Brainstorm at least 3 subject lines for each email.

Gist of Email Content	Subject Line(s)

Goal/Call to Action in Email	Send Date	Outline	Draft	Edit	Scheduled
		○	○	○	○
		○	○	○	○
		○	○	○	○
		○	○	○	○
		○	○	○	○
		○	○	○	○
		○	○	○	○
		○	○	○	○
		○	○	○	○
		○	○	○	○
		○	○	○	○
		○	○	○	○
		○	○	○	○
		○	○	○	○
		○	○	○	○
		○	○	○	○
		○	○	○	○
		○	○	○	○
		○	○	○	○
		○	○	○	○
		○	○	○	○

MONTH AT A GLANCE

SUNDAY	MONDAY	TUESDAY	WEDNESDAY

Plug your tasks, key dates and projects for the month into the overview.
Are you doing a sprint? Block it off in the calendar.

THURSDAY	FRIDAY	SATURDAY	NOTES

REVIEW YOUR MONTH

	This Month	Last Month	+/- Change
Email Subscribers			
Pageviews			
Bounce Rate			
5 Most Popular Posts (In Google Analytics)			
Average session time			
Top 5 Traffic Refferers			

Track each of your emails sent out this month.

Subject Line	Open Rate	Click Rate

Revenue Source	Amount
Total	

Expenses	Amount
Total	

	This Month	Last Month	+/- Change
f			
(twitter)			
(instagram)			
in			
g+			
p			
(youtube)			

Track each post for the month and how well it did on two of your most important social media platforms. Track the number of opt-ins each content upgrade received.

Posts	Social Shares	Content Upgrade Opt-ins	Comments

REVIEW YOUR QUARTER 2

What worked well for you this quarter?

How can you replicate these results?

What obstacles are you facing in achieving your goals? Why is it difficult?

Did this quarter help you get closer to your annual objectives?

What can you try to overcome them?

List Your Top 5 Most Popular Content Upgrades for this Quarter	Subscribers

Let's review your content strategy for the quarter:

Do you see any patterns in the type of posts that attract an audience to your blog?

How can you capitalize on the success of these posts? (Example: Add content upgrades, develop a related product, create similar posts, repurpose existing posts)

Let's review your email strategy for the quarter:

Do you see any patterns in the type of subject lines that worked well for your list?

Which emails received the most engagement and replies from your list? Can you tell why?

What opt-in incentive is working in terms of conversion rate? Keep it status quo or change it up?

_____

_____

_____

_____

Do you need to clean your list? (Re-engage or delete subscribers who haven't opened or clicked on your emails in 3 months or more)

_____

_____

_____

_____

Do you need to make changes to how your website is optimized? (E.g. Any posts with lots of traffic buy not converting to subscribers? Do you need to add extra opt-in forms? Do you need to add testimonials to a landing page?)

_____

_____

_____

_____

Are there any emails with a high unsubscribe rate? Can you tell why?

_____

_____

_____

Do you see any patterns in the type of content upgrades that get the most opt-ins?

_____

_____

_____

Where did most subscribers come from?

_____

_____

_____

PLAN YOUR QUARTER 3

What blogging stage are you in?

Stage 1 Stage 2 Stage 3 Stage 4

○   ○   ○   ○

List 3 goals you want to achieve by the end of this quarter. Does every goal help you reach your stage milestone? If it doesn't, rethink your goal.

GOAL 1 ....

LIST EVERY TASK YOU CAN THINK OF TO COMPLETE YOUR GOAL

GOAL 2 ....

LIST EVERY TASK YOU CAN THINK OF TO COMPLETE YOUR GOAL

GOAL 3 ....

LIST EVERY TASK YOU CAN THINK OF TO COMPLETE YOUR GOAL

List any key projects and their deadlines for this quarter

Project	Deadline	Sprint Y/N	Tentative Sprint Dates

LET'S PLAN MONTH:

List 3 things you hope to achieve by the end of the month?

GOAL 1

LIST EVERY TASK YOU CAN THINK OF TO COMPLETE YOUR GOAL

GOAL 2

LIST EVERY TASK YOU CAN THINK OF TO COMPLETE YOUR GOAL

GOAL 3

LIST EVERY TASK YOU CAN THINK OF TO COMPLETE YOUR GOAL

List All Maintenance Tasks
for the Month

○ ....
○ ....
○ ....
○ ....
○ ....
○ ....
○ ....
○ ....
○ ....

List All Marketing Tasks
for the Month

○ ....
○ ....
○ ....
○ ....
○ ....
○ ....
○ ....
○ ....
○ ....

List All Project Tasks for the Month

○ ....   ○ ....
○ ....   ○ ....
○ ....   ○ ....
○ ....   ○ ....

List Important Dates for the Month

List all launch dates, affiliate promotions, collaborations, sales etc.

○ ....   ○ ....
○ ....   ○ ....
○ ....   ○ ....
○ ....   ○ ....

What content would support your goals for this month?

What content upgrades would complement these posts?

What content do you plan to publish this month?

Include any audios and videos as well. Plot your content ideas into this table.

Date	Title	Format
14.03.18	Why you need a content plan: 5 Steps to Create your brilliant content plan	Blog post

Goal of Content	Content Upgrade	Outline	Draft	Edit	Publish
Awareness - why a content plan is important	Checklist	○	○	⊗	○
		○	○	○	○
		○	○	○	○
		○	○	○	○
		○	○	○	○
		○	○	○	○
		○	○	○	○
		○	○	⊗	○
		○	○	○	○
		○	○	○	○
		○	○	○	○
		○	○	⊗	○
		○	○	○	○
		○	○	○	○
		○	○	○	○
		○	○	○	○
		○	○	○	○
		○	○	○	○
		○	○	⊗	○
		○	○	○	○
		○	○	○	○
		○	○	○	○
		○	○	○	○
		○	○	○	○

What emails will you send this month?

Think about the type of email content that will support your goals for this month.
Brainstorm at least 3 subject lines for each email.

Gist of Email Content	Subject Line(s)

Goal/Call to Action in Email	Send Date	Outline	Draft	Edit	Scheduled
		○	○	○	○
		○	○	○	○
		○	○	○	○
		○	○	○	○
		○	○	○	○
		○	○	○	○
		○	○	○	○
		○	○	○	○
		○	○	○	○
		○	○	○	○
		○	○	○	○
		○	○	○	○
		○	○	○	○
		○	○	○	○
		○	○	○	○
		○	○	○	○
		○	○	○	○
		○	○	○	○
		○	○	○	○
		○	○	○	○
		○	○	○	○

MONTH AT A GLANCE

SUNDAY	MONDAY	TUESDAY	WEDNESDAY

Plug your tasks, key dates and projects for the month into the overview.
Are you doing a sprint? Block it off in the calendar.

THURSDAY	FRIDAY	SATURDAY	NOTES

REVIEW YOUR MONTH

	This Month	Last Month	+/- Change
Email Subscribers			
Pageviews			
Bounce Rate			
5 Most Popular Posts (In Google Analytics)			
Average session time			
Top 5 Traffic Refferers			

Track each of your emails sent out this month.

Subject Line	Open Rate	Click Rate

Revenue Source	Amount
Total	

Expenses	Amount
Total	

	This Month	Last Month	+/- Change
f			
(twitter)			
(instagram)			
in			
g+			
(pinterest)			
(youtube)			

Track each post for the month and how well it did on two of your most important social media platforms. Track the number of opt-ins each content upgrade received.

Posts	Social Shares	Content Upgrade Opt-ins	Comments

LET'S PLAN MONTH:

List 3 things you hope to achieve by the end of the month?

GOAL 1

LIST EVERY TASK YOU CAN THINK OF TO COMPLETE YOUR GOAL

GOAL 2

LIST EVERY TASK YOU CAN THINK OF TO COMPLETE YOUR GOAL

GOAL 3

LIST EVERY TASK YOU CAN THINK OF TO COMPLETE YOUR GOAL

List All Maintenance Tasks for the Month

○ ....
○ ....
○ ....
○ ....
○ ....
○ ....
○ ....
○ ....
○ ....

List All Marketing Tasks for the Month

○ ....
○ ....
○ ....
○ ....
○ ....
○ ....
○ ....
○ ....
○ ....

List All Project Tasks for the Month

○ ....   ○ ....
○ ....   ○ ....
○ ....   ○ ....
○ ....   ○ ....

List Important Dates for the Month

List all launch dates, affiliate promotions, collaborations, sales etc.

○ ....   ○ ....
○ ....   ○ ....
○ ....   ○ ....
○ ....   ○ ....

What content would support your goals for this month?

What content upgrades would complement these posts?

YOUR CREATE SPACE

What content do you plan to publish this month?

Include any audios and videos as well. Plot your content ideas into this table.

Date	Title	Format

Goal of Content	Content Upgrade	Outline	Draft	Edit	Publish
		○	○	○	○
		○	○	○	○
		○	○	○	○
		○	○	○	○
		○	○	○	○
		○	○	○	○
		○	○	○	○
		○	○	○	○
		○	○	○	○
		○	○	○	○
		○	○	○	○
		○	○	○	○
		○	○	○	○
		○	○	○	○
		○	○	○	○
		○	○	○	○
		○	○	○	○
		○	○	○	○
		○	○	○	○
		○	○	○	○
		○	○	○	○
		○	○	○	○
		○	○	○	○
		○	○	○	○
		○	○	○	○

What emails will you send this month?

Think about the type of email content that will support your goals for this month.
Brainstorm at least 3 subject lines for each email.

Gist of Email Content	Subject Line(s)

Goal/Call to Action in Email	Send Date	Outline	Draft	Edit	Scheduled
		○	○	○	○
		○	○	○	○
		○	○	○	○
		○	○	○	○
		○	○	○	○
		○	○	○	○
		○	○	○	○
		○	○	○	○
		○	○	○	○
		○	○	○	○
		○	○	○	○
		○	○	○	○
		○	○	○	○
		○	○	○	○
		○	○	○	○
		○	○	○	○
		○	○	○	○
		○	○	○	○
		○	○	○	○
		○	○	○	○
		○	○	○	○
		○	○	○	○

MONTH AT A GLANCE

SUNDAY	MONDAY	TUESDAY	WEDNESDAY

Plug your tasks, key dates and projects for the month into the overview.
Are you doing a sprint? Block it off in the calendar.

THURSDAY	FRIDAY	SATURDAY	NOTES

REVIEW YOUR MONTH

	This Month	Last Month	+/- Change
Email Subscribers			
Pageviews			
Bounce Rate			
5 Most Popular Posts (In Google Analytics)			
Average session time			
Top 5 Traffic Refferers			

Track each of your emails sent out this month.

Subject Line	Open Rate	Click Rate

Revenue Source	Amount
Total	

Expenses	Amount
Total	

	This Month	Last Month	+/- Change
f			
(twitter)			
(instagram)			
in			
g+			
(pinterest)			
(youtube)			

Track each post for the month and how well it did on two of your most important social media platforms. Track the number of opt-ins each content upgrade received.

Posts	Social Shares	Content Upgrade Opt-ins	Comments

LET'S PLAN MONTH:

List 3 things you hope to achieve by the end of the month?

GOAL 1

LIST EVERY TASK YOU CAN THINK OF TO COMPLETE YOUR GOAL

GOAL 2

LIST EVERY TASK YOU CAN THINK OF TO COMPLETE YOUR GOAL

GOAL 3

LIST EVERY TASK YOU CAN THINK OF TO COMPLETE YOUR GOAL

List All Maintenance Tasks for the Month

○ ....
○ ....
○ ....
○ ....
○ ....
○ ....
○ ....
○ ....
○ ....

List All Marketing Tasks for the Month

○ ....
○ ....
○ ....
○ ....
○ ....
○ ....
○ ....
○ ....
○ ....

List All Project Tasks for the Month

○ ....   ○ ....
○ ....   ○ ....
○ ....   ○ ....
○ ....   ○ ....

List Important Dates for the Month

List all launch dates, affiliate promotions, collaborations, sales etc.

○ ....   ○ ....
○ ....   ○ ....
○ ....   ○ ....
○ ....   ○ ....

What content would support your goals for this month?

What content upgrades would complement these posts?

YOUR CREATE SPACE

What content do you plan to publish this month?

Include any audios and videos as well. Plot your content ideas into this table.

Date	Title	Format

Goal of Content	Content Upgrade	Outline	Draft	Edit	Publish
		◯	◯	◯	◯
		◯	◯	◯	◯
		◯	◯	◯	◯
		◯	◯	◯	◯
		◯	◯	◯	◯
		◯	◯	◯	◯
		◯	◯	◯	◯
		◯	◯	◯	◯
		◯	◯	◯	◯
		◯	◯	◯	◯
		◯	◯	◯	◯
		◯	◯	◯	◯
		◯	◯	◯	◯
		◯	◯	◯	◯
		◯	◯	◯	◯
		◯	◯	◯	◯
		◯	◯	◯	◯
		◯	◯	◯	◯
		◯	◯	◯	◯
		◯	◯	◯	◯
		◯	◯	◯	◯
		◯	◯	◯	◯
		◯	◯	◯	◯
		◯	◯	◯	◯

What emails will you send this month?

Think about the type of email content that will support your goals for this month.
Brainstorm at least 3 subject lines for each email.

Gist of Email Content	Subject Line(s)

Goal/Call to Action in Email	Send Date	Outline	Draft	Edit	Scheduled
		◯	◯	◯	◯
		◯	◯	◯	◯
		◯	◯	◯	◯
		◯	◯	◯	◯
		◯	◯	◯	◯
		◯	◯	◯	◯
		◯	◯	◯	◯
		◯	◯	◯	◯
		◯	◯	◯	◯
		◯	◯	◯	◯
		◯	◯	◯	◯
		◯	◯	◯	◯
		◯	◯	◯	◯
		◯	◯	◯	◯
		◯	◯	◯	◯
		◯	◯	◯	◯
		◯	◯	◯	◯
		◯	◯	◯	◯
		◯	◯	◯	◯
		◯	◯	◯	◯
		◯	◯	◯	◯

MONTH AT A GLANCE

SUNDAY	MONDAY	TUESDAY	WEDNESDAY

Plug your tasks, key dates and projects for the month into the overview.
Are you doing a sprint? Block it off in the calendar.

THURSDAY	FRIDAY	SATURDAY	NOTES

REVIEW YOUR MONTH

	This Month	Last Month	+/- Change
Email Subscribers			
Pageviews			
Bounce Rate			
5 Most Popular Posts (In Google Analytics)			
Average session time			
Top 5 Traffic Refferers			

Track each of your emails sent out this month.

Subject Line	Open Rate	Click Rate

Revenue Source	Amount
Total	

Expenses	Amount
Total	

	This Month	Last Month	+/- Change
f			
Twitter			
Instagram			
LinkedIn			
g+			
Pinterest			
YouTube			

Track each post for the month and how well it did on two of your most important social media platforms. Track the number of opt-ins each content upgrade received.

Posts	Social Shares	Content Upgrade Opt-ins	Comments

NOTES

REVIEW YOUR QUARTER 3

What worked well for you this quarter?

How can you replicate these results?

What obstacles are you facing in achieving your goals? Why is it difficult?

Did this quarter help you get closer to your annual objectives?

What can you try to overcome them?

List Your Top 5 Most Popular Content Upgrades for this Quarter	Subscribers

Let's review your content strategy for the quarter:

Do you see any patterns in the type of posts that attract an audience to your blog?

How can you capitalize on the success of these posts? (Example: Add content upgrades, develop a related product, create similar posts, repurpose existing posts)

_____

_____

_____

_____

_____

_____

Let's review your email strategy for the quarter:

Do you see any patterns in the type of subject lines that worked well for your list?

_____

_____

_____

_____

_____

_____

Which emails received the most engagement and replies from your list? Can you tell why?

_____

_____

_____

_____

_____

_____

What opt-in incentive is working in terms of conversion rate? Keep it status quo or change it up?

_____

_____

_____

_____

Do you need to clean your list? (Re-engage or delete subscribers who haven't opened or clicked on your emails in 3 months or more)

_____

_____

_____

_____

Do you need to make changes to how your website is optimized? (E.g. Any posts with lots of traffic buy not converting to subscribers? Do you need to add extra opt-in forms? Do you need to add testimonials to a landing page?)

_____

_____

_____

_____

Are there any emails with a high unsubscribe rate? Can you tell why?

_____

_____

_____

Do you see any patterns in the type of content upgrades that get the most opt-ins?

_____

_____

_____

Where did most subscribers come from?

_____

_____

_____

PLAN YOUR QUARTER 4

What blogging stage are you in?

Stage 1   Stage 2   Stage 3   Stage 4

List 3 goals you want to achieve by the end of this quarter. Does every goal help you reach your stage milestone? If it doesn't, rethink your goal.

GOAL 1

LIST EVERY TASK YOU CAN THINK OF TO COMPLETE YOUR GOAL

GOAL 2

LIST EVERY TASK YOU CAN THINK OF TO COMPLETE YOUR GOAL

GOAL 3 ....

LIST EVERY TASK YOU CAN THINK OF TO COMPLETE YOUR GOAL

List any key projects and their deadlines for this quarter

Project	Deadline	Sprint Y/N	Tentative Sprint Dates

LET'S PLAN MONTH:

List 3 things you hope to achieve by the end of the month?

GOAL 1

LIST EVERY TASK YOU CAN THINK OF TO COMPLETE YOUR GOAL

GOAL 2

LIST EVERY TASK YOU CAN THINK OF TO COMPLETE YOUR GOAL

GOAL 3

LIST EVERY TASK YOU CAN THINK OF TO COMPLETE YOUR GOAL

List All Maintenance Tasks for the Month

○ ....
○ ....
○ ....
○ ....
○ ....
○ ....
○ ....
○ ....
○ ....

List All Marketing Tasks for the Month

○ ....
○ ....
○ ....
○ ....
○ ....
○ ....
○ ....
○ ....
○ ....

List All Project Tasks for the Month

○ ....   ○ ....
○ ....   ○ ....
○ ....   ○ ....
○ ....   ○ ....

List Important Dates for the Month

List all launch dates, affiliate promotions, collaborations, sales etc.

○ ....   ○ ....
○ ....   ○ ....
○ ....   ○ ....
○ ....   ○ ....

YOUR CREATE SPACE

What content would support your goals for this month?

What content upgrades would complement these posts?

YOUR CREATE SPACE

What content do you plan to publish this month?

Include any audios and videos as well. Plot your content ideas into this table.

Date	Title	Format

Goal of Content	Content Upgrade	Outline	Draft	Edit	Publish
		○	○	○	○
		○	○	○	○
		○	○	○	○
		○	○	○	○
		○	○	○	○
		○	○	○	○
		○	○	○	○
		○	○	○	○
		○	○	○	○
		○	○	○	○
		○	○	○	○
		○	○	○	○
		○	○	○	○
		○	○	○	○
		○	○	○	○
		○	○	○	○
		○	○	○	○
		○	○	○	○
		○	○	○	○
		○	○	○	○
		○	○	○	○
		○	○	○	○
		○	○	○	○
		○	○	○	○

What emails will you send this month?

Think about the type of email content that will support your goals for this month.
Brainstorm at least 3 subject lines for each email.

Gist of Email Content	Subject Line(s)

Goal/Call to Action in Email	Send Date	Outline	Draft	Edit	Scheduled
		○	○	○	○
		○	○	○	○
		○	○	○	○
		○	○	○	○
		○	○	○	○
		○	○	○	○
		○	○	○	○
		○	○	○	○
		○	○	○	○
		○	○	○	○
		○	○	○	○
		○	○	○	○
		○	○	○	○
		○	○	○	○
		○	○	○	○
		○	○	○	○
		○	○	○	○
		○	○	○	○
		○	○	○	○
		○	○	○	○
		○	○	○	○

MONTH AT A GLANCE

SUNDAY	MONDAY	TUESDAY	WEDNESDAY

Plug your tasks, key dates and projects for the month into the overview.
Are you doing a sprint? Block it off in the calendar.

THURSDAY	FRIDAY	SATURDAY	NOTES

REVIEW YOUR MONTH

	This Month	Last Month	+/- Change
Email Subscribers			
Pageviews			
Bounce Rate			
5 Most Popular Posts (In Google Analytics)			
Average session time			
Top 5 Traffic Refferers			

Track each of your emails sent out this month.

Subject Line	Open Rate	Click Rate

Revenue Source	Amount
Total	

Expenses	Amount
Total	

	This Month	Last Month	+/- Change
f			
🐦			
📷			
in			
g+			
📌			
▶			

Track each post for the month and how well it did on two of your most important social media platforms. Track the number of opt-ins each content upgrade received.

Posts	Social Shares	Content Upgrade Opt-ins	Comments

LET'S PLAN MONTH:

List 3 things you hope to achieve by the end of the month?

GOAL 1

LIST EVERY TASK YOU CAN THINK OF TO COMPLETE YOUR GOAL

GOAL 2

LIST EVERY TASK YOU CAN THINK OF TO COMPLETE YOUR GOAL

GOAL 3

LIST EVERY TASK YOU CAN THINK OF TO COMPLETE YOUR GOAL

List All Maintenance Tasks for the Month

○ ....

○ ....

○ ....

○ ....

○ ....

○ ....

○ ....

○ ....

○ ....

List All Marketing Tasks for the Month

○ ....

○ ....

○ ....

○ ....

○ ....

○ ....

○ ....

○ ....

○ ....

List All Project Tasks for the Month

○ ....   ○ ....

○ ....   ○ ....

○ ....   ○ ....

○ ....   ○ ....

List Important Dates for the Month

List all launch dates, affiliate promotions, collaborations, sales etc.

○ ....   ○ ....

○ ....   ○ ....

○ ....   ○ ....

○ ....   ○ ....

What content would support your goals for this month?

What content upgrades would complement these posts?

YOUR CREATE SPACE

YOUR CREATE SPACE

What content do you plan to publish this month?

Include any audios and videos as well. Plot your content ideas into this table.

Date	Title	Format

Goal of Content	Content Upgrade	Outline	Draft	Edit	Publish
		◯	◯	◯	◯
		◯	◯	◯	◯
		◯	◯	◯	◯
		◯	◯	◯	◯
		◯	◯	◯	◯
		◯	◯	◯	◯
		◯	◯	◯	◯
		◯	◯	◯	◯
		◯	◯	◯	◯
		◯	◯	◯	◯
		◯	◯	◯	◯
		◯	◯	◯	◯
		◯	◯	◯	◯
		◯	◯	◯	◯
		◯	◯	◯	◯
		◯	◯	◯	◯
		◯	◯	◯	◯
		◯	◯	◯	◯
		◯	◯	◯	◯
		◯	◯	◯	◯
		◯	◯	◯	◯
		◯	◯	◯	◯
		◯	◯	◯	◯
		◯	◯	◯	◯
		◯	◯	◯	◯

What emails will you send this month?

Think about the type of email content that will support your goals for this month.
Brainstorm at least 3 subject lines for each email.

Gist of Email Content	Subject Line(s)

Goal/Call to Action in Email	Send Date	Outline	Draft	Edit	Scheduled
		○	○	○	○
		○	○	○	○
		○	○	○	○
		○	○	○	○
		○	○	○	○
		○	○	○	○
		○	○	○	○
		○	○	○	○
		○	○	○	○
		○	○	○	○
		○	○	○	○
		○	○	○	○
		○	○	○	○
		○	○	○	○
		○	○	○	○
		○	○	○	○
		○	○	○	○
		○	○	○	○
		○	○	○	○
		○	○	○	○
		○	○	○	○

MONTH AT A GLANCE

SUNDAY	MONDAY	TUESDAY	WEDNESDAY

Plug your tasks, key dates and projects for the month into the overview.
Are you doing a sprint? Block it off in the calendar.

THURSDAY	FRIDAY	SATURDAY	NOTES

REVIEW YOUR MONTH

	This Month	Last Month	+/- Change
Email Subscribers			
Pageviews			
Bounce Rate			
5 Most Popular Posts (In Google Analytics)			
Average session time			
Top 5 Traffic Refferers			

Track each of your emails sent out this month.

Subject Line	Open Rate	Click Rate

Revenue Source	Amount
Total	

Expenses	Amount
Total	

	This Month	Last Month	+/- Change
f			
(twitter)			
(instagram)			
in			
g+			
(pinterest)			
(youtube)			

Track each post for the month and how well it did on two of your most important social media platforms. Track the number of opt-ins each content upgrade received.

Posts	Social Shares	Content Upgrade Opt-ins	Comments

LET'S PLAN MONTH:

List 3 things you hope to achieve by the end of the month?

GOAL 1

LIST EVERY TASK YOU CAN THINK OF TO COMPLETE YOUR GOAL

GOAL 2

LIST EVERY TASK YOU CAN THINK OF TO COMPLETE YOUR GOAL

GOAL 3

LIST EVERY TASK YOU CAN THINK OF TO COMPLETE YOUR GOAL

List All Maintenance Tasks for the Month

○ ....
○ ....
○ ....
○ ....
○ ....
○ ....
○ ....
○ ....
○ ....

List All Marketing Tasks for the Month

○ ....
○ ....
○ ....
○ ....
○ ....
○ ....
○ ....
○ ....
○ ....

List All Project Tasks for the Month

○ ....   ○ ....
○ ....   ○ ....
○ ....   ○ ....
○ ....   ○ ....

List Important Dates for the Month

List all launch dates, affiliate promotions, collaborations, sales etc.

○ ....   ○ ....
○ ....   ○ ....
○ ....   ○ ....
○ ....   ○ ....

What content would support your goals for this month?

What content upgrades would complement these posts?

YOUR CREATE SPACE

What content do you plan to publish this month?

Include any audios and videos as well. Plot your content ideas into this table.

Date	Title	Format

Goal of Content	Content Upgrade	Outline	Draft	Edit	Publish
		○	○	○	○
		○	○	○	○
		○	○	○	○
		○	○	○	○
		○	○	○	○
		○	○	○	○
		○	○	○	○
		○	○	○	○
		○	○	○	○
		○	○	○	○
		○	○	○	○
		○	○	○	○
		○	○	○	○
		○	○	○	○
		○	○	○	○
		○	○	○	○
		○	○	○	○
		○	○	○	○
		○	○	○	○
		○	○	○	○
		○	○	○	○
		○	○	○	○
		○	○	○	○
		○	○	○	○

What emails will you send this month?

Think about the type of email content that will support your goals for this month.
Brainstorm at least 3 subject lines for each email.

Gist of Email Content	Subject Line(s)

Goal/Call to Action in Email	Send Date	Outline	Draft	Edit	Scheduled
		○	○	○	○
		○	○	○	○
		○	○	○	○
		○	○	○	○
		○	○	○	○
		○	○	○	○
		○	○	○	○
		○	○	○	○
		○	○	○	○
		○	○	○	○
		○	○	○	○
		○	○	○	○
		○	○	○	○
		○	○	○	○
		○	○	○	○
		○	○	○	○
		○	○	○	○
		○	○	○	○
		○	○	○	○
		○	○	○	○
		○	○	○	○

MONTH AT A GLANCE

SUNDAY	MONDAY	TUESDAY	WEDNESDAY

Plug your tasks, key dates and projects for the month into the overview.
Are you doing a sprint? Block it off in the calendar.

THURSDAY	FRIDAY	SATURDAY	NOTES

REVIEW YOUR MONTH

	This Month	Last Month	+/- Change
Email Subscribers			
Pageviews			
Bounce Rate			
5 Most Popular Posts (In Google Analytics)			
Average session time			
Top 5 Traffic Refferers			

Track each of your emails sent out this month.

Subject Line	Open Rate	Click Rate

Revenue Source	Amount
Total	

Expenses	Amount
Total	

	This Month	Last Month	+/- Change
f			
twitter			
instagram			
in			
g+			
p			
youtube			

Track each post for the month and how well it did on two of your most important social media platforms. Track the number of opt-ins each content upgrade received.

Posts	Social Shares	Content Upgrade Opt-ins	Comments

NOTES

REVIEW YOUR QUARTER 4

What worked well for you this quarter?

How can you replicate these results?

What obstacles are you facing in achieving your goals? Why is it difficult?

Did this quarter help you get closer to your annual objectives?

What can you try to overcome them?

List Your Top 5 Most Popular Content Upgrades for this Quarter	Subscribers

Let's review your content strategy for the quarter:

Do you see any patterns in the type of posts that attract an audience to your blog?

How can you capitalize on the success of these posts? (Example: Add content upgrades, develop a related product, create similar posts, repurpose existing posts)

_____

_____

_____

_____

_____

Let's review your email strategy for the quarter:

Do you see any patterns in the type of subject lines that worked well for your list?

_____

_____

_____

_____

_____

_____

Which emails received the most engagement and replies from your list? Can you tell why?

_____

_____

_____

_____

_____

_____

What opt-in incentive is working in terms of conversion rate? Keep it status quo or change it up?

_____

_____

_____

_____

Do you need to clean your list? (Re-engage or delete subscribers who haven't opened or clicked on your emails in 3 months or more)

_____

_____

_____

_____

Do you need to make changes to how your website is optimized? (E.g. Any posts with lots of traffic buy not converting to subscribers? Do you need to add extra opt-in forms? Do you need to add testimonials to a landing page?)

_____

_____

_____

_____

Are there any emails with a high unsubscribe rate? Can you tell why?

_____

_____

_____

Do you see any patterns in the type of content upgrades that get the most opt-ins?

_____

_____

_____

Where did most subscribers come from?

_____

_____

_____

YOUR CREATE SPACE
Inspiration for Your next 12 month

YOUR CREATE SPACE

BECAUSE TO FOLLOW A CALLING REQUIRES WORK. IT'S HARD. IT HURTS. IT DEMANDS ENTERING THE PAIN-ZONE OF EFFORT, RISK, AND EXPOSURE.

– STEVEN PRESSFIELD, TURNING PRO

YOU MADE IT TO THE END!

Building a blog and business is challenging.

It takes courage to chase your dreams and determination to show up every single day. It won't be easy but your work *will* inspire and touch several others.

When you find yourself detracting from your goals, slipping into your old routines or feeling overwhelmed, keep your 'why' front and center. Take it one task a day and you'll be much further along in a month than if you never started. Focus on your journey and stop comparing it to someone else's middle.

Before you go, remember to download your bonuses at **CREATEPLANNER.COM/BONUS**

Good luck and thank you for sharing your work with the world!

If you want to get in touch, come find me here at my slice of the internet: **www.meerakothand.com**

I can't wait to see what you create and I'm rooting for you!

ABOUT THE AUTHOR

Meera is a certified email marketing specialist, blogger and a self-professed email nerd. She writes over at Meerakothand.com where she helps bloggers and solopreneurs create authentic businesses minus the sleaze to build an unmissable, stand out online presence.

Her speciality: Simplifying marketing strategy with no-fluff, direct and actionable advice to rid you of frustration and overwhelm. She has been featured on Smart Blogger, Marketing Profs, YFS, Addicted 2 Success and several other sites.

Connect with Meera @**meerakothand**

Made in the USA
Lexington, KY
09 December 2018